THE EU,
ETHNIC
MINORITIES
AND
MIGRANTS
IN THE
WORKPLACE

THE EU, ETHNIC MINORITIES AND MIGRANTS IN THE WORKPLACE

John Wrench

KOGAN PAGE

First published in 1998

Kogan Page Limited
120 Pentonville Road
London N1 9JN

Concise yet comprehensive, the Dossiers present accessible analysis of EU policies, institutions and related themes. Written by experts in the field and commissioned by the London European Research Centre of the University of North London, the European Dossiers are an invaluable source of information and interpretations for anyone with an interest in the EU.

Published five times per year, the Dossiers are available through an annual subscription or as individual titles.

Comments on the series or proposals for new titles are welcome in writing to the series editor:

Professor Michael Newman
London European Research Centre
University of North London
166–220, Holloway Road
London N7 8DB

British Library Cataloguing in Publication Data

ISBN 0 7494 2605 5

Typeset by JS Typesetting, Wellingborough, Northants.
Printed and bound in Great Britain by
Biddles Ltd, Guildford and King's Lynn

Contents

Biographical Notes

Dr John Wrench is a Senior Researcher at the Danish Centre for Migration and Ethnic Studies, South Jutland University Centre. Prior to that he worked at the Centre for Research in Ethnic Relations, University of Warwick. He has researched and published for many years in the area of labour market discrimination and exclusion in the UK and in the European Union, and has in recent years been commissioned to carry out research for the UK Department for Education and Employment, the International Labour Office, and the European Foundation for the Improvement of Living and Working Conditions. Recent publications include *Racism and Migration in Western Europe* (Oxford 1993, edited with John Solomos), *Preventing Racism at the Workplace* (Luxembourg 1996) and *European Compendium of Good Practice for the Prevention of Racism at the Workplace* (Luxembourg 1997).

European Dossier Series: Editorial Board

1

Formal and Informal Discrimination in Employment in the EU

This Dossier first considers the evidence for both formal discrimination and informal racial or ethnic discrimination in employment in European Union member states. This discrimination adversely affects the opportunities of migrant workers, as well as their descendants, who are no longer migrants. The Dossier goes on to look at the implications of this discrimination for policy and practice, both at an EU and member state level. Perhaps the most obvious implication of this evidence is that of the need for legal measures against discrimination, at both levels. However, action on this is slow to come, largely because of political opposition from various national governments. It is therefore more realistic in the short term to expect some progress to be made in policies to tackle informal racial discrimination – policies at the organisational, rather than national or European, level. The final section of this Dossier, therefore, looks critically at evidence on initiatives against racism and discrimination in employment which have recently been introduced in both public and private sector organisations in various European countries, showing how the character and emphasis of these initiatives vary widely across EU member states, and attempting some explanation for this variation. The indications are that actions against racism and discrimination at the organisational level remain rather 'tame', with employers slow to recognise that in some circumstances there can be positive business or efficiency advantages in such actions. The conclusion is that employers need more legal 'encouragement' before they will act, and that nationally the likelihood of this will be enhanced by pressure from the European level.

BACKGROUND

In the post war period of employment boom, immigrant workers were encouraged to enter Europe to cover labour shortages. Since the early 1970s the decline in the old manufacturing industries, which previously employed immigrants, meant that they were disproportionately affected by redundancies. Since the 1970s most European countries have consistently demonstrated significantly higher rates of unemployment for immigrants and ethnic minorities who have originated from outside the EU, and this is particularly noticeable for the second and third generations who were born, or had most of their education, in Europe.

The reasons for the exclusion of immigrant and ethnic minority people from the labour market, or their over-representation in precarious and 'atypical' work, are many. They are often living in the wrong areas, away from newly-created employment opportunities, and the young people often leave school with fewer qualifications than their indigenous peers. However, they also suffer other exclusions. In some countries they are victims of certain forms of legal exclusion which persist against non-EU citizens and reduce their employment opportunities, and in all countries they are vulnerable to the more 'informal' exclusion which results from direct and indirect discrimination, regardless of educational attainment.

This Dossier shows how different forms of exclusion affect the migrant and ethnic minority population in different ways, according to their legal status within a country, and demonstrates the operation of these two kinds of exclusion: formal or legal discrimination and informal or racial discrimination. The formal restrictions in the labour market experienced by migrants without full citizenship rights are well known, and have led to calls for changes in policy at EU level, as well as the extension of citizenship or denizenship[1] rights at member state level (Layton-Henry 1990; Wrench 1996). What is less generally accepted is the widespread existence of informal racial discrimination which leads to the exclusion of groups of people from the employment opportunities they deserve. The concealed nature of these processes of discrimination leads to the danger of underestimating the extent of the problem.

Chapter 1 of this Dossier considers in turn the mechanisms of legal exclusion, and the processes of racial discrimination, which operate simultaneously in western European labour markets.

LEGAL CATEGORIES OF WORKER IN THE EU

The working population of the EU can be divided into five main categories in terms of legal status (Wrench 1996 p3)

1. citizens living and working within their own country of citizenship
2. citizens of an EU member state who work in another country within the Union (EU denizens)
3. third country nationals who have full rights to residency and work in a member state (non-EU denizens)
4. third country nationals who have leave to stay on the basis of a revocable work permit for a fixed period of time
5. undocumented or 'illegal' workers.

---

[1] A denizen is a foreign citizen with full rights to residence and work, and substantial social rights – see Hammar 1990.

The above categories reflect formal status and a continuum of rights ranging from full rights and privileges of citizenship in group 1 to virtually no rights in group 5. As group 1 workers have full social, political and employment rights, the concept of legal or formal discrimination does not apply here. In theory, group 2 workers – citizens of an EU member state who work in another country within the Union – should also experience no formal discrimination. However in practice, in some countries certain positions remain effectively closed even to white nationals of other EU countries, despite the inclusion of the concept of 'European Citizenship' in the Treaty of Maastricht. The problem here is with those countries which still in practice restrict the access to at least some of their public sector jobs. In Greece, by law, the overwhelming majority of public sector jobs are reserved for Greek nationals, with no more than a few dozen nationals of other EU countries being employed in the broader public sector. In other EU member states such as Belgium and France, exclusion operates by administrative practice rather than at a formal level, so that although in theory EU denizens have equal access to public sector jobs such as teaching, in practice this is rare. In Luxembourg public sector jobs are barred to other EU citizens. One case which recently came to public attention was that of a Spanish national who was refused permission to sit a competitive examination organised by the National Museum of History and Art (Kollwelter 1995). Accordingly, the European Commission instituted an action against the Luxembourg Government on the grounds that it had not fulfilled its obligations under the Treaty of Rome.

The above examples are anomalies, in that in theory free access to employment for any citizen of an EU member state should exist. However, the formal barriers to opportunities are far more of a problem for the groups of workers lower down in the hierarchy of categories.

FORMAL AND LEGAL DISCRIMINATION AGAINST NON-EU NATIONALS

There are two main ways in which the rights of group 3 workers – third country nationals who have full rights to residency and work in a member state – are restricted with regard to employment. Firstly, they are restricted in their freedom to find work in other member states. Secondly, they are excluded from certain categories of jobs within the member state in which they live.

Lack of freedom to find work in other member states

The inclusion of European citizenship in the Treaty of Maastricht gave citizens of EU countries the right to move freely within and between member states in search of employment. However, nationals of non-member countries are excluded from these rights, even though they may be established, legally-resident workers of long standing. An example of the negative effect of such restriction can be seen with the closure of old industries which formerly employed large numbers of migrants. After redundancy, EU denizens are able to look for new work in neighbouring countries, whereas non-EU denizens do not have that option. The clearest example is perhaps that of the Limbourg coal mines in Campine in Belgium which were closed down in 1987/88. This closure affected some 5800 workers, a significant proportion of whom were Italian (13 per cent) and Turkish (10 per cent). Two years after the closure, 82 per cent of Belgian miners had found another job. By contrast, 30 per cent of Italian miners and 83 per cent of Turkish miners were still unemployed. Some 78 per cent of Turkish miners had not worked at all since the closure of the coal mines (Denolf and Martens 1991). One of the extra disadvantages faced by the Turkish miners in comparison with the other two groups was that they were not free to find work over the borders in neighbouring countries.

Exclusion from certain sectors of work

There are, however, not only problems for non-EU denizens who wish to cross borders to look for work. There are also restrictions on the jobs they may apply for *within* their country of residence. In France a large number of jobs in the public sector – gas and electricity utilities, the state railways, the Paris transport undertaking, etc. apply the rule of excluding foreigners other than EU nationals. Three and a half million national and local government jobs and two and a half million jobs in nationalised or similar undertakings are thus closed to foreigners other than EU nationals (De Rudder et al 1995). In the Netherlands public sector employers are allowed to discriminate against non-nationals in a limited number of cases: Dutch nationality is explicitly required for high ranking posts in the judiciary, the military, the police and the diplomatic service, and in positions involving state security (Zegers de Beijl 1995). In Greece the public sector, as already mentioned, is overwhelmingly reserved for Greek nationals. Even in the teaching profession very few foreigners are employed in the state schools. Consequently, almost all of the roughly 26,000 foreigners with work permits are employed in the private sector of the economy. Non-Greek citizens cannot chair any trade union, federation or labour centre (Fakiolas 1995). In Portugal foreign nationals are prohibited from taking public office other than on the authorisation of the minister responsible for the sector. There is also a restriction on the employment of foreign nationals in another sense: a company with more than five employees can only employ foreign nationals as long as the level of their Portuguese employees remains at 90 per cent. Since foreign workers tend to be concentrated in certain limited sectors, this provision has encouraged the development of illegal work. The 10 per cent ceiling can be exceeded if justified by reasons of 'public interest' (Carlos and Borges 1995).

Whereas the legally-based insecurities described above are certainly problematic for non-EU denizens, there are even greater problems for those third country nationals whose freedom is constrained by the need for a fixed-term work permit. This leads us to consider the fourth group of workers and the particular restrictions they face.

Third country nationals on temporary permits

Workers in group 4 – third country nationals who have leave to stay on the basis of a revocable work permit for a fixed period of time – are not citizens or denizens of the country where they reside and work. These are similar in position to those in category 3, but with fewer rights and a weaker position in the labour market. Category 3 workers often began as workers in this category. A permit may be held for a number of months for a restricted activity or geographical area, or for several years, for any activity or area. Some from this group will, over time, fall into category 5 of 'illegal' workers when they remain in the country after their permit runs out or they take work in a field not covered by their existing permit.

Probably the best illustration of problems faced by this group of workers is in Austria, a country where the legal discrimination operating against migrant workers through national policy is so comprehensive that it overshadows any discrimination which might operate at the informal level. An array of legal instruments establishes substantial legal inequality between foreign nationals and Austrians in the labour market (Gächter 1995). Foreign nationals, in order to be an active part of the labour force, require both a residence permit and a labour market permit. There are four different kinds of labour market permits, none of them permanent. Access to the labour market is tightly controlled. The law sets an absolute ceiling on the foreign labour force – at the time of writing, nine per cent of the total labour force. Ceilings are regularly reached, meaning that no new permits can be issued. This leaves many legally-resident people without the possibilty of legal employment.

Among other things, the system leads to unemployment patterns unlike those for migrant workers in other European countries, with foreign nationals in Austria exhibiting *lower* unemployment rates than Austrian wage earners, and with the unemployment rate *increasing* for those with less restrictive work permits. These patterns can be explained by looking at the effects of the legal restrictions in operation. If a third-country national becomes unemployed, he or she will not be entitled to unemployment benefit for the same period of time as Austrian citizens, with the most common duration of benefits for third-country nationals being only 30 weeks. Once benefits run out and no new employment has been found, or if a new Employment Permit has not been granted and there are no other sources of income, the right to reside in the country is lost. Further residence may be tolerated for the time being but it will be based on a visa that does not permit access to the labour market. There will be no access to legal employment or any kind of legal income (Gächter 1995).

The shortened duration of insurance benefits, and the exclusion from legal income it leads to, put serious pressure on foreign nationals. Regardless of the kind of permit they hold, they are under pressure to find new employment quickly in order to escape the threat of becoming 'illegal'. Thus they have to accept whatever conditions are offered in order not to remain unemployed for too long. The result is the absence of long-term unemployment observed in the statistics, but also a systematic allocation of foreign workers to the worst occupations (Gächter 1995).

effects of such legal inequality are compounded gal restriction. Foreign nationals, although from voting in works council elections, are be elected to them. This deprives them of the opportunity to bargain over issues such as wages, working hours and working conditions. Since foreign and Austrian workers do not often work side by side, but tend to be concentrated in different occupations within one plant which are either spatially or hierarchically segregated, there are sections and strata of the workforce that tend not to be represented. All this has the effect of placing foreign workers not only under pressure to accept jobs with poor working conditions, arbitrary hours and low pay, but also to have to remain compliant within them. Foreign nationals are therefore very attractive to employers as a relatively powerless and highly flexible workforce. Consequently, foreign nationals are a preferred category of employees for unskilled and semi-skilled occupations without customer contact (Gächter 1995).

Although workers in the EU on temporary permits are legal and therefore in theory have access to the protection of laws on working conditions, in practice this protection is not always easy to draw upon. In Spain, for example, Cachón (1995) argues that many legal immigrants are subjected to similar conditions to those of illegal immigrants: they work with no contract or social security benefits, with lower wages and/or longer working days than allowed by union agreements in that sector. Even if the immigrants are 'regular', they are always subject to the annual five-year renewal of their work permit and are therefore in an institutionalised situation of temporary employment and residence which restricts their bargaining power.

Undocumented or 'illegal' workers

Group 5 workers range from recent political refugees whose status has not been recognised, to people who have worked in the EU for many years without any legal rights to residence or employment. Illegal employment can sometimes result in a move to legal employment, perhaps through marriage, by filing an asylum application, or during a general regularisation campaign (see Groen-endijk and Hampsink 1995 p102).

The illegal labour market is said to be expanding in EU countries, particularly from the eastern borders. However, the main problem of illegal labour remains in the countries of the south. In Greece, undocumented foreigners are employed by smaller firms which are usually family undertakings and can avoid labour inspections and social insurance contributions (Fakiolas 1995). The undocumented economic immigrants are estimated at over 350,000, about eight to nine per cent of the registered labour force of 4.1m. They are not covered by social insurance, and their pay is about half of the market rate in Greece.

'Illegal' immigrants were estimated to represent 40–60 per cent of all immigrant (non-EU) workers in Spain at the end of 1993. With no contract or social security benefits, they often suffer exploitative working conditions in terms of wages, quality, intensity or duration of their work, practices which violate regulations and Union agreements. Employers in certain sectors prefer to employ such immigrants because of their low cost, pliability and vulnerability. Employers have the advantage of holding absolute power over their employees, since illegal immigrants cannot make formal complaints or take legal action (Cachón 1995).

In Italy, data collected by the Ispettorato del Lavoro reveal differences between north and south in the various economic sectors which use illegal labour. In central and northern Italy, the industrial sector and the hotel and catering trade have the most 'illegal' workers, whereas in southern Italy and the islands, there is more undeclared employment in the agricultural sector. In the agricultural sector, particularly in the south, employment is insecure, temporary and/or seasonal and is rarely covered by trade union protection as regards pay and working conditions (Campani et al 1995).

In Portugal, many foreign workers are found in unskilled work earning far below average pay without a contract or social security coverage, and unable to challenge their employers over poor working conditions, or to seek work elsewhere. About 50 per cent of ethnic minority workers have no employment contract, with no legal protection, welfare rights, or protection against abuses of safety or working hours. Work accidents are highest in those sectors which employ migrants (Carlos and Borges 1995).

Thus the legal insecurities of group 5 workers mean that they suffer the worst forms of employment conditions. The issue of discrimination is perceived differently in this context than in northern countries. It concerns the super-exploitation of large numbers of migrants suffering conditions which would not be tolerated by native workers, but which they are not in a position to reject. They are recruited because of their low cost and reduced powers of resistance to exploitation, which is a direct result of their legal status.

INFORMAL OR RACIAL DISCRIMINATION

This section of the Dossier looks at how employment experiences are determined not by legal status, but by the operation of processes at the informal level. Even those people with full and formal citizenship rights can suffer disadvantage in the labour market on the grounds of ethnic background and colour, not to mention national origin or religious affiliation. However, within many European countries there is still a reluctance to acknowledge that racial discrimination operates, and that full citizenship rights for a non-white national do not accord protection (Wrench and Solomos 1993). Unlike legal discrimination, this sort of exclusion is more difficult to recognise – it operates through acts of discrimination at an individual level which collectively build up to ensure that the opportunities of whole groups of people are severely undermined. There are sometimes open acts of racism which are recognised by those who experience them, but which may be difficult to demonstrate to others. More commonly, racial discrimination operates quietly and is not even recognised by the victims.

Indirect evidence for discrimination

Discrimination in employment can be said to occur when migrants/ethnic minorities are accorded inferior treatment in the labour market or in the workplace, relative to nationals/whites, despite being comparably qualified in terms of education, experience or other relevant criteria. There are a number of ways that we can gain evidence for the operation of discrimination in the labour market. Some of this evidence is only *indirect*. For example, in the US, comparisons of the earnings of black and white men who are equal in terms of education, experience and other relevant factors, shows that black men earn about 85–90 per cent of the earnings of their white counterparts. The gap is assumed to be attributable to discrimination (Burstein 1992 p906). Similar indirect evidence can be found in European countries. For example, in the Netherlands, after holding constant other variables, such as education, age, sex, occupational level, and region, several researchers have still found a discrepancy in large data sets between the unemployment figures of native Dutch and those of ethnic minorities (Veenman 1990; Kloek 1992; Speller and Willems 1990). A similar example from the UK comes from a nationally-representative sample of 28,000 young people who were first eligible to leave school in 1985 and 1986 (Drew et al 1992). Even after taking account of factors such as attainment and local labour market conditions, young people from ethnic minorities were found to be more likely to experience both higher rates and longer spells of unemployment. In Sweden statistical patterns point to discrimination on the basis of country of origin affecting the success of refugees finding work. When other factors are held constant, refugees from Eastern Europe and Latin America are found to do better than refugees from Iran, Iraq, Africa, the Far East and the Middle East (Soininen and Graham 1995).

Direct evidence for discrimination

It is also possible to get *direct* evidence of racial discrimination through discrimination testing. The method of discrimination testing seems to have first been used in the UK, and has since been adopted by researchers in many other countries. The method utilises two or more testers, one belonging to a majority group and the others to minority ethnic groups, all of whom apply for the same jobs. The testers are matched for all the criteria which should normally be taken into account by an employer, such as age, qualifications, experience and schooling. If over a period of repeated testing the applicant from the majority background is systematically preferred to the others, then this points to the operation of discrimination according to ethnic background (Bovenkerk 1992).

In the UK, researchers acting in the guise of young applicants from ethnic minority backgrounds applied by letter for non-manual jobs advertised in the local paper of one English city (Hubbuck and Carter 1980). Matching letters of application were sent to each employer advertising a vacancy from three test candidates, one native white, one Afro-Caribbean and one Asian. Where all three candidates were called for an interview, this was seen by the researchers to be 'non-discrimination'. In fact in 48 per cent of the cases the Afro-Caribbean or Asian applicant was refused interview whilst the white applicant was called for interview, whereas in only 6 per cent of the cases did the reverse happen.

In the Netherlands, Bovenkerk and Breunig-van Leeuwen (1978), using this method, had two equally qualified applicants from different ethnic backgrounds respond to the same vacancy, and found that employers gave greater preference to the native Dutch person. Recently this research was repeated, on the authority of the International Labour Organisation (ILO) as part of the ILO's ongoing programme 'Combating discrimination against (im)migrant workers and ethnic minorities in the world of work'. Discrimination was tested against Moroccan and Surinamese applicants, when applying for semi-skilled jobs and when applying for jobs requiring a college education (Bovenkerk et al 1995). At the lower job level, discrimination was encountered by both ethnic groups, by males as well as females, in one out of three applications. At higher levels, the outcome was less pronounced as in one out of five applications, preference was given to the native Dutch men. No discrimination could be demonstrated against college-educated non-native women. In the private sector, discrimination occurred twice as often as it did in the public sector.

The method of discrimination testing is one of the most important and effective means of demonstrating the existence of the problem area in the face of those who deny that discrimination occurs. Unfortunately, although the method has been used in countries such as Canada and the US, it has still not been widely applied in other EU countries. In certain countries – Sweden, for example – the method has been deemed to be in breach of rules guiding research ethics. However, under the ILO programme, similar research has been promoted in a number of other EU countries, including Germany, Spain, Belgium and Denmark. Initial findings show that net discrimination rates of around 35 per cent are not uncommon (Goldberg et al 1995; Colectivo IOE 1996; Hjarnø and Jensen 1997).

Qualitative research into discrimination

Qualitative research can give an insight into what lies behind the direct labour market exclusion revealed in discrimination testing. Such research can at times discover open prejudice, directly expressed. In the Netherlands, interviews with employers demonstrated prejudices against foreign employees, despite the fact that employers and personnel managers are unlikely to be completely candid and open to researchers about their actions (Gras and Bovenkerk 1995). Van Beek (1993) reported that as many as 80 per cent of personnel managers interviewed gave preference to an applicant with a Dutch background, in the case of equally qualified applicants, and that 20 per cent thought a person from an ethnic minority would be completely unacceptable.

In a recent study in Norway, 160 managers representing the 400 largest Norwegian firms were interviewed (*Økonomisk rapport* 1995, cited in Rogstad 1995). Almost eight out of ten managers thought that managers in Norway do discriminate against immigrants in the recruitment process. They were asked what they thought were the three main reasons for this. The answers indicate that 'difference in culture' was regarded as the most important reason (60 per cent). But also 'not having a knowledge of the language' (59 per cent), 'uncertainty about their formal qualifications' (35 per cent), 'xenophobia' (26 per cent) and 'racism and negative attitudes towards foreigners' (22.4 per cent), all featured as reasons (Rogstad 1995). Some French employers interviewed by De Rudder et al (1995) systematically refused to recruit persons from North Africa and Africa generally, offering no justification other than, for example, 'I already have one black on my site; I don't want two, because then they get difficult to handle.' Some employers interviewed in the UK made plain their prejudices, labelling West Indians as 'lethargic', or having a 'laissez-faire approach', or 'not very mechanical'. Pakistani boys had 'a lack of technical language . . . a lack of mechanical curiosity'; Asians were 'weak in mechanical design'. One engineering manager said 'the West Indians fit in better. The Asians have funny food. We don't want the whites disturbed by funny practices' (Lee and Wrench 1983).

More often employers will claim that their actions are determined not by their own prejudices but by the prejudices of others. Hjarnø (1995) describes an interview with the owner of a company in Denmark engaged in plumbing work. He argued that he was not a racist at a personal level – however, he would not employ immigrants and refugees. The main reason was that some of his customers would object to having a tradesman of foreign origin coming into their house and doing maintenance or other types of work on behalf of his firm. He was convinced he would lose customers if he took on immigrants and refugees, and he felt that in his trade, very few firms would take on foreigners, even as apprentices.

Research done in the UK similarly described employers who would argue that it was not they themselves who were prejudiced, but that they had to take account of the prejudices of others, such as their workforce or their customers. Employers recruiting young people for apprenticeship training described 'no go areas' in their firms, where white workers would refuse to work with a black trainee, and these tended to be skilled areas of work (Lee and Wrench 1983). Officials who assisted school leavers to find work encountered employers who said they didn't want Asian girls for shop assistants because 'it's not right for our customers', or that they were a high class store and 'it may affect the selling' (Cross et al 1990).

In France, De Rudder et al (1995) described employers who justify their unwillingness to take on applicants by claiming that the other employees at the plant will not work with foreigners or 'coloured' people, that the employment of immigrants 'would detract from the firm's image', or that persons whose foreign origin is 'visible' cannot be employed in situations where they have to be in contact with the public.

Informal criteria in recruitment

Sometimes the prejudices of employers are not expressed directly, but can be teased out from certain statements and practices which are expressed in more socially acceptable ways. Many of these fall under the heading of informal criteria in recruitment and selection decisions. Jenkins (1986) contrasted the 'suitability' of applicants – their educational and technical qualifications, with their 'acceptability' – the more informal and subjectively judged characteristics on which recruiters form judgements as to whether someone will 'fit in' to the organisation. In a study of UK companies Jewson and Mason (1991) found that technical qualifications would be regarded as first screening devices, with much importance given to 'acceptability' criteria in making the final selections. It is precisely the criteria of 'acceptability' where negative racial and ethnic stereotypes come into play.

In the Netherlands, socially normative criteria, such as the motivation and reliability of the applicant and fitting into the team, appear to be becoming more important factors in the selection of personnel than technically instrumental criteria, such as education and work experience (Verweij 1991). Something similar is described by De Rudder et al (1995), who found evidence that recruitment procedures in France have evolved in the direction of placing more and more emphasis on personal interviews, at the expense of written tests. Employers now take it upon themselves to examine the 'personality' of job applicants, their personal opinions and aspects of their lives which have increasingly little to do with their vocational aptitudes (Lyon-Caen 1992). This change is particularly marked in the civil service, which used to take pride in recruiting staff on the basis of anonymous, 'competitive' written examinations.

In Sweden, Soininen and Graham (1995) describe the expansion of new types of job which require communication skills, especially a good command of Swedish and a high level of education, as well as 'social competence'. They also involve the delegation of responsibility, a stress upon individual initiative and a greater reliance on teamwork. However, some authorities saw this as an understandable justification for not employing immigrants. In the words of the Swedish Immigrant Policy Committee Report (SOU 1995):

All special treatment on the basis of cultural difference need not be discrimination. In today's companies the demand for social competence is increasing, i.e. the demand that employees, regardless of whether they are Swedes or immigrants, fit into the work culture, function in a team, etc. Knowledge of and familiarity with functioning in a Swedish environment can be assumed to be an important part of such competence. This means that an employer can take account of certain factors when employing [someone] which disqualify cultural difference. It is obvious that the dividing line between justifiable demands for social competence and what is discrimination can be difficult to establish.

Soininen and Graham (1995) find fault with this line of argument, pointing out that similar arguments were employed in earlier years to block the entry of women to male-dominated working places. Today, they argue, the Swedish Law on Equal Opportunity does not allow this kind of 'cultural argument' to be used as a barrier to women's participation on the same terms as men, and such arguments should be similarly unjustifiable for immigrants.

Indirect discrimination

Indirect discrimination in employment exists with job requirements or recruitment practices which, although applied equally to all, in practice treat members of one ethnic group more favourably than another. The exclusion resulting from indirect discrimination can be either accidental or intentional. Practices which led to indirect discrimination were revealed in a UK study of access to apprenticeships (Lee and Wrench 1983). For example, many firms relied for recruitment in a significant part on the family members of existing employees, and trade unions would often support this policy. Thus, in a largely white workforce, this excluded ethnic minorities. Furthermore, many employers restricted their recruitment to a local catchment area when faced with a large number of applicants. As the largest employers were located in white outer suburbs of cities, this excluded ethnic minority applicants from the beginning.

Examples of such factors are found in reports on other European countries. The selective use of white geographical areas for recruitment is also reported in France (De Rudder et al 1995). Recruitment through the family and friends of the company's own personnel was seen to lead to indirect discrimination in the Netherlands (Veenman 1985; Becker and Kempen 1982; Abell et al 1985; Bovenkerk 1986). This has also been reported in Portugal (Carlos and Borges 1995), Denmark (Hjarnø, 1995), and Germany (Schaub 1993). The recruitment methods most commonly used in Finland are said to be network, informal and internal recruitment. One estimate is that employment agencies in Finland are informed about less than 30 per cent of vacancies (Ekholm and Pitkänen 1995). In Sweden, the use of family ties, friends and acquaintances accounts for filling 70 per cent of vacancies, according to a study by AMS (AMS 1991; Paulson 1991). Thus, newly-arrived immigrants are at a clear disadvantage if their only means of finding work is through the employment services. De Rudder et al (1995) describe the approach adopted by certain nationalised enterprises in France, where preference for the children of staff is described as an 'unwritten law', widely subscribed to and often encouraged by the trade unions. One informant stated that 80 per cent of contracts offered by a public transport enterprise in the Paris region under the Emploi Solidarité scheme had been placed in this way. Another, more unusual, example of indirect discrimination, described in the Netherlands, concerns the minimum height demand for entry to some occupations (eg the armed forces and the police). Those who are indirectly harmed by these demands are those ethnic minority groups who are, on average, smaller in height than the indigenous population.

With indirect discrimination it is not easy to come to a judgement as to whether its effects are truly inadvertent, or whether the exclusion is intentional. This no doubt varies. With long-established criterion such as minimum height, the exclusion effect is likely to be unintentional. The demand for minimum language skills is a genuine criterion for many occupations; however, where apparently unnecessary language skills are required for many un-skilled jobs, one is more likely to be suspicious. The discriminatory effects of a decision to restrict recruitment to a particular region or catchment area which excludes migrants and ethnic minorities is likely to be quite obvious to a recruiter, and this is far less likely to be accidental in its effects.

THE INTERACTION OF FORMAL AND INFORMAL DISCRIMINATION

The five categories of worker set out at the beginning of this Dossier reflect formal status, and a continuum of rights ranging from full rights and privileges of citizenship in category 1 to virtually negligible rights in category 5. New gradations of inequality are then added to these legal differences in the form of visible minority status. According to the interaction of these formal and informal criteria, workers in the different groups have different experiences of discrimination and exclusion.

In the first two categories, EU citizens living in their own country, and EU citizens working in another EU member state, non-white groups form only a minority. In the next three categories they are more likely to form a majority. In all categories the non-white workers are likely to suffer disadvantage at least relative to the white members of that legal category. Paradoxically, the relative disadvantage suffered through racial discrimination for workers in categories 1, 2 and to a lesser extent, 3, constitutes a more visible social issue precisely because they have more formal rights. They have justifiable expectations of fair and equal treatment and are more likely to be in positions where they are in competition with white workers in the labour market. An increasing proportion of visible minorities within these categories will have been born and educated in an EU country. Further down the hierarchy, it becomes less easy to demonstrate the extent to which the relative disadvantage in employment experience is a result of racial or ethnic discrimination, partly because the disadvantage on formal and legal grounds is greater and more obvious, and because workers in these categories are less likely to be competing with white nationals in the same labour market. By the time we get to the category 5 workers in the illegal labour market, it is difficult to separate out the effects of racism from the straightforward exploitation of a relatively powerless group of workers. To talk about racial discrimination in the conventional sense is less appropriate as these workers are often in a different labour market from full citizens. Nevertheless, it is clear that racist beliefs can be drawn upon as an ideology of justification for the exploitation which occurs at this level. Furthermore, there are often differences according to colour in the circumstances of those engaged in the illegal labour market: Poles working illegally on building sites in Germany or Belgium do not suffer the intensely degrading and exploitative near-slavery conditions of some of the non-European agricultural workers in Spain.

This chapter has demonstrated the existence of unjustifiable discrimination of a formal and informal kind, Chapter 2 now considers the policy implications of this evidence, both at an EU and a member state level.

2

The Policy Implications at EU and Member State Level

The implications of the arguments and evidence presented in this paper so far are that action is necessary to tackle both the formal legal discrimination and informal racial discrimination which occurs against migrant and ethnic minority workers in the EU. The action against each needs to be taken both at the EU level and at individual member state level, as follows:

Table 1

	Measures against legal discrimination	Measures against racial discrimination
EU level	improvement of rights of third country nationals	EU directive on racial discrimination
		Code of Practice/Joint Declaration of Social Partners
Member state level	improvement of citizenship rights	anti-discrimination laws 'voluntary' measures at an organisational level

MEASURES AGAINST LEGAL DISCRIMINATION

EU level: Improvement of the rights of third-country nationals

The first issue is that of the anomalous status of third country nationals in the EU, and the discrimination and disadvantage related to this.

> *It is difficult . . . to justify a two-tier workforce – one with the right to work anywhere in the EC, and the other restricted to a single EC country* (Dummett 1994, p19).

The European Commission's view is that an internal market without frontiers, in which the free movement of persons is ensured, logically implies the free movement of all legally resident third-country nationals for the purpose of engaging in economic activities, and that this objective should be realised progressively. Although there was a commitment to provide for the free movement of all EU residents, at the Edinburgh summit in December 1992, there was little subsequent movement to implement this (Mirza 1995). As a CRE report puts it:

> *The distinction between EC nationals and legally resident third-country nationals carries real dangers. As the single market develops there will be more opportunities for jobs, business and cultural activity, but third-country nationals will not be able to move in order to take advantage of them. In fact, the more the Community offers, the greater their disadvantage. The gap between them and their EC national neighbours can only widen unless their legal rights are improved throughout the EC* (Dummett 1994 p28).

We have seen many examples in this Dossier of the ways in which this disadvantage is experienced. There were hopes that the Draft Treaty of Amsterdam in 1997 would bring significant advance. The 'Migrants Forum' of the EU had campaigned for the Treaty to extend European citizenship rights to third-country nationals who have been living legally in the EU for more than five years. However, this did not happen. In November 1997 the European Commission did adopt a proposal for a Council of Ministers' regulation extending the right to third country nationals legally residing in one member state to move between member states without losing their social security entitlements. However, the Commission emphasised that this proposal did not imply granting the right to free movement under EU law to third-country nationals (*Migration News Sheet*, Brussels, December 1997).

Member state level: Improvement of citizenship rights

The process of the formation of the EU has led to a more intensive reflection on the nature of citizenship as a concept, and more practically, to debates on the merits of extending citizenship rights within the EU (see Bauböck 1992). In those countries where it is not easy to achieve citizenship, there are employment disadvantages which are unacceptable, particularly when this applies to legally-resident people born in the country of migrant parents. It is difficult to talk about measures against racism and discrimination when a barrier to improving this situation is the legal status of the population of migrant origin. Moreover, an 'open' citizenship policy can also be seen as an important symbolic step, because it recognises the increasing heterogeneity in the country's population and incorporates migrants politically and legally on an equal basis. Lack of full rights is a symbolic form of exclusion which can only add to the alienation of ethnic minority young people who are made to feel that they are not full members of society.

There are a number of European states where natural-isation is not easy, and this could, and should, be rectified.

Nevertheless, it must be realised that even when natural-isation is made easier, the inclination of migrants to apply for naturalisation has often remained relatively low, particularly when this has necessitated giving up their citizenship of origin. This has been the case, for example, in Germany. Recently, the Turkish Government has made it easier for their nationals to retain many of their rights in Turkey if they give up their Turkish nationality and take up German citizenship, and there is evidence that young Turkish people are opting for German nationality in increasing numbers.[2] Nevertheless, even in this case, there are still arguments for the right to *dual* citizenship. Scholars suggest that after decades in which migrants have been 'differentially incorporated' into a nation state they tend to develop strong ethnic structures and an ethnic identity. Therefore, the giving up of the original citizen-ship might be regarded within ethnic communities as 'an abandonment of national identities' (Bauböck 1992). In addition, according to some commentators, many migrants reject the idea of being exclusively German and thus a member of a community which they feel rejects and discriminates against them (Brandt, forthcoming).

The situation with regard to dual citizenship in Germany is in fact more complicated than it initially seems. The German Government's line is that dual or multiple citizen-ship is something to be avoided and officially discouraged. However, in practice, dual citizenship is tolerated on a large scale. For one thing, dual citizenship emerges 'naturally'. It has been estimated that the marriages of Germans to 'foreigners' between 1950–1990 could produce between one and two million children with poten-tial dual citizenship. In addition to this, the Aussiedler, or ethnic Germans, are allowed to keep their original citizenship when naturalised. Therefore, scholars have

---

[2] Interview with Birgit Brandt, University of Warwick, researching issues of citizenship amongst Turks in Berlin in 1988.

argued that the official government opposition to dual citizenship begins to look somewhat selective, not so much based on an issue of principle and international law, but rather reflecting a resistance to the naturalisation of permanently settled migrants (Brandt, forthcoming). As long as dual citizenship is formally discouraged the percentage of naturalisation of migrant workers will remain low. This means that the migrant population is not only discriminated against in everyday life, but also by legislation, which prohibits employers from employing migrants without an EU nationality, so long as EU nationals can be found.

The examples quoted in this Dossier of German and Austrian legal and administrative barriers to the equal treatment of migrant workers are perhaps the most visible and extreme examples of a more general point which is applicable to many other countries. Where rules exist which make it difficult for migrants – including second generation migrants – to be regarded as equal in the labour market, these legal discriminations would need to be removed before other anti-discrimination measures could become fully effective.

Some scholars argue that we may not necessarily have to think in terms of full citizenship as such, in the removal of legal barriers. Layton-Henry (1990 p194) writes:

Foreign residents who live in a country for longer than a temporary stay gradually become members of their country of residence, and this fact should be recognised, even if most may not want to become naturalised citizens of their new society. We suggest that a new status of denizenship should be granted to them, entitling them to all the rights of citizenship within their country of residence, including the right to participate in national elections. This would give them rights similar to those of dual nationals, who have rights in more than one country.

Forbes and Mead, in their 1992 review of measures to combat discrimination in EU member states, argue that voting rights transform an outsider pressure group into a significant bloc of potential voters, given the way that visible minority groups tend to be concentrated in urban areas, and ensure increased access to the political process. This has the long-term effect of altering the agenda of political parties. Thus 'the lack of voting and full citizenship rights is a very good indicator of the absence of adequate legislation dealing with racial discrimination' (Forbes and Mead 1992 p74).

There are still those who think that the extension of citizenship (or denizenship) rights is all that is needed to ameliorate the disadvantaged situation of migrant workers in Europe. Brandt (forthcoming), when discussing the concept of citizenship in the context of German debates on the integration of migrants, warns that we should be realistic about this.

> *Without denying the importance of changing citizenship politics in Germany, the limits of such a policy have to be taken into consideration: formal membership – although one instrument – is by no means a guarantee of 'equal opportunity' or an answer to a society divided along ethnic/racial lines – clearly, France and Britain illustrate this point.*

Arguments which focus only on the formal rights of citizenship fail to recognise the relevance of racial or ethnic discrimination to social disadvantage. Hence the need for simultaneous measures against informal or racial discrimination.

MEASURES AGAINST INFORMAL OR RACIAL DISCRIMINATION

EU level: Directive on racial discrimination

Across EC countries, measures to combat discrimination vary in their scope and effectiveness, and in some cases hardly exist. Many member states are at quite different stages of developing law and practice to deal with racial discrimination in employment:

> *It is clear that protection within individual states against racial discrimination is wholly inadequate and that it will take many years for states to summon the requisite will to introduce measures which are truly effective. In order to realise fully the aim of the Single Market and in order to allow for the free movement of workers . . . in pursuit of that aim, legislation at the European level is both desirable and necessary* (Mirza 1995 p62).

The argument had been advanced that the Treaty of Rome and the Single European Act did not confer any competence on the Union in the field of racial or ethnic discrimination, with the assumption that measures against racial discrimination should remain the concern only of individual member states. Others have argued that there are good reasons why action at EU level is important. Mirza concludes that there are arguments that legislation at Community level is justified because race discrimination is an issue of a transnational nature and will not be adequately tackled at state level. The lack of Community action, combined with the erratic nature of protection against racial discrimination at state level, conflicts with the requirements of the Treaty to correct distortions of competition and to strengthen social cohesion; and action at Community level, because of its standardising effect, would prove beneficial to an extent that is not possible if action were taken at member state level (Mirza 1995 p61).

A committee of experts appointed after the EU Corfu summit in June 1994 produced a report in 1995 recommending the amendment of the Maastricht Treaty to provide explicitly for Community competence on discrimination against migrants and ethnic minorities, in the same way that it covers sex discrimination. It recommends directives and regulations at Community level to cover issues which include discrimination in employment. An EU directive sets out certain goals which have to be met by a given deadline. Each member state must then pass the necessary laws:

> *Protection against discrimination in the member states needs to include elements that are common to the whole Community – so that there is some uniform protection throughout the EC. But complete uniformity would be impossible, given the different legal systems and conditions in the 12 countries. A directive is therefore the ideal instrument laying down a common basis in firm goals to be achieved through legislation but allowing each national government the flexibility to deal with its own particular problems* (Dummett 1994 p14).

The obligations of the Equal Treatment Directive led to every EU country introducing legislation to guarantee equal treatment between men and women in the labour market (Forbes and Mead 1992). The same should now be done for racial discrimination:

> *By its very existence, European sex equality law recognises the need to interfere with the operation of 'free' market forces. It is a major inconsistency in European policy that legal protection is available to address the unequal treatment of women workers, but that parallel provisions are not available for racial and minority ethnic groups.*

There is no evidence to suggest that the cost advantages to employers from discriminating on grounds of race are any less than for sex discrimination (Sales and Gregory 1995 p5).

The 1997 Draft Treaty of Amsterdam saw some progress on this, when a clause was introduced – Article 13 – which for the first time allows the European institutions to take action to combat discrimination based on a range of criteria, including racial or ethnic origin. However, the Migrants Forum of the EU remained critical of the Treaty because no specific provision was established to ensure the implementation of measures against discrimination.[3]

EU level: Code of practice/Joint declaration of social partners

Codes of good practice against discrimination in employment are currently in use in the UK and the Netherlands. A code gives guidance to help employers and others to understand the law, and sets out policies which can be implemented to help to eliminate racial discrimination and enhance equality of opportunity in the workplace. A code can give practical guidance to explain the implications of a country's anti-discrimination legislation, and can recommend measures to reduce the possibility of unlawful behaviour occurring. Although a code itself does not impose legal obligations and only has advisory status, it is possible that failure to observe its recommendations could result in breaches of the law. In the UK, evidence about compliance with the code's recommendations can be taken into account by industrial tribunals in deciding whether an act of unlawful discrimination has occurred

---

[3] At the time of writing, plans for European legislation outlawing racism and discrimination in employment (and in other arenas) were being put before the European Commission, in a document which stated that 'the transnational dimension of the problems justifies action at a European level' (*Guardian* 25 March 1998).

and assessing the degree of liability by employers for any such acts.

In order to encourage the adoption of such a code at member state level it would be possible for the EU to initiate a code of practice to combat racial discrimination in employment, similar to the code it initiated on sexual harassment. Such a code could cover the full range of employment issues, such as recruitment and selection procedures, opportunities for training and promotion, disciplinary procedures for racial harassment, dismissal and redundancy procedures, and taking account of particular cultural or religious needs. A code could encourage organisations to adopt an equal opportunity policy, and anti-discrimination training for staff. There might be variation in codes so that different codes could be drawn up to relate specifically to trade unions and employment agencies, as in the Netherlands.

The July 1994 White Paper (*European Social Policy: A Way Forward for the Union*) stated the Commission's intention to consult the social partners at European level on the possible adoption of a code of good employment practice against racial discrimination. The Commission asked the European Human Rights Foundation to put together a draft document to serve as a basis for discussions between the social partners. This draft, entitled *A Code of Practice to Combat Racial Discrimination and to Promote Equal Opportunities at Work* was produced in 1994 (Coussey and Hammelburg 1994).

However, as of yet the EU social partners have failed to agree on a common code of practice. As a first stage, at the Social Dialogue Summit in Florence in October 1995, they agreed instead on a *Joint Declaration on the Prevention of Racial Discrimination and Xenophobia and Promotion of Equal Treatment at the Workplace*. This sets out a range of means that can make a positive contribution towards preventing racial discrimination at the workplace, and encourages employers and trade unions to adopt such measures (See Section 3).

Member state level: Anti-discrimination legislation

There have been several recent comparative analyses of the workings of national anti-discrimination law, and of enforcement agencies, in Europe in the 1990s, generally coming down in favour of strengthening and extending legal measures at a national level (Zegers de Beijl 1991; Forbes and Mead 1992; CEC 1993; MacEwen 1995; MacEwen 1997). Existing international conventions on racial discrimination, such as the ILO Convention 111 on Discrimination in Employment and Occupation, are seen to have substantive effects only when they lead to and inform domestic legislation on discrimination (Forbes and Mead 1992). A starting principle of domestic legislation is to make racial discrimination a criminal and/or a civil offence. Although in some countries racial discrimination in employment is covered by criminal law, many commentators are not convinced that this is the best way of countering it. Whereas racist attacks, harassment and propaganda are threats to public order and these can be dealt with by criminal law, civil proceedings may be more effective for racial discrimination. This occurs for a number of reasons, including the fact that the standard of proof is less rigorous, and that in civil law the applicant can initiate proceedings, whereas it is usually only the police who initiate criminal proceedings (Banton 1994).

Banton points to France, where the primary remedy for all kinds of discrimination lies in criminal law. Statistics show that by 1991 the annual number of convictions had risen to 101, almost entirely for offences against public order, namely for incitement to racial hatred, insult, and so on. There were just four convictions for racial discrimination in employment. This 'scarcely suggests that criminal remedies are effective in this field.' For Banton, the French experience shows that while criminal law can be effective in dealing with racial defamation by the published word, as in the press, it is ineffective in dealing with discrimination in the workplace. (Some other countries rely on labour law to combat workplace discrimination; however, this leaves the victim dependent upon support from a trade union.) British experience suggests that remedies in civil law are more effective. Forbes and Mead (1992) argue that 'racial discrimination can be a criminal *and* civil offence, thereby opening up two quite different avenues for the aggrieved individual, with important implications for the educative effect of convictions'.

Member state level: Voluntary measures at an organisational level

Experience in the US shows that anti-discrimination legislation is a necessary but not sufficient means of reducing racial discrimination in employment. The effect of such legislation is often for racism to become more subtle, and that indirect, institutional or unintentional discrimination becomes more important. Therefore, as well as enacting laws against discrimination, member states should encourage a range of social policy initiatives against racism and discrimination at an organisational level, including equal opportunities programmes, codes of practice, positive action, education and information provision, and training. The law can be used not just to prohibit, but to allow, to encourage and to facilitate. It can provide a stimulus for organisations to undertake voluntary action, such as adopting equal opportunity policies. An equal opportunities policy consists of a set of aims and procedures adopted by an organisation which should be summarised in a public statement and made known to all employees. An equal opportunities policy could include:

- ethnic monitoring of job applicants;
- equality targets for recruitment and entry to management posts;

- recruitment initiatives to encourage ethnic minority applicants;
- training for recruiters and selectors on avoiding racial discrimination;
- positive action measures to stimulate ethnic minority applications; and
- procedures against racial harassment.

In the same way that an EU directive on racial discrimination would act as a stimulus for the introduction of legislation at member state level, the EU's *Joint Declaration on the Prevention of Racial Discrimination and Xenophobia and Promotion of Equal Treatment at the Workplace* acts as a stimulus to voluntary actions at an organisational level. The declaration proposes a set of follow-up measures, among them the compilation of a Compendium of Good Practice, to encourage further voluntary actions[4] in organisations across European member states. Therefore, during 1996–1997 researchers in all 15 EU countries were asked to seek out case studies of good practice in the employment of migrants and combating racism and discrimination, and these were compiled in the *European Compendium of Good Practice*, published towards the end of 1997 (Wrench 1997). The *Compendium* reveals a tremendous variety between the different member states in the emphasis and character of the initiatives which exist. These different approaches are described and analysed in the final section of this Dossier.

---

[4] Although such policies are generally defined as 'voluntary', in practice some will be introduced through the latent pressure of legislation and the fear by some organisations of the bad publicity which might ensue from a court or tribunal case on discrimination.

3

Measures at an Organisational Level Found in EU Member States

The objectives of the *European Compendium of Good Practice* were set out in the 1995 Joint Declaration on the Prevention of Racial Discrimination and Xenophobia and Promotion of Equal Treatment at the Workplace. These include:

- identifying examples of good practice in the different member states;
- disseminating the information gathered, contributing to a broader exchange of experiences amongst the members of the EU;
- providing guidance to all interested parties (ie employers, workers, trade unions, employers' organisations and employment services) regarding the promotion of equal treatment and the combating of racial discrimination at the workplace;
- promoting the notion that it is in the interests of business to implement equal opportunities policies.

The *European Compendium of Good Practice for the Prevention of Racism* at the Workplace (Wrench 1997) includes 25 case studies from the 15 countries of the EU. The case studies encompass private and public sector companies, trade unions, collective agreements, codes of conduct and national initiatives. This section summarises the main practices described in the Compendium and attempts an analysis of the reasons for the differences in character of the various initiatives adopted by organisations in EU countries.

EXAMPLES OF 'GOOD PRACTICE'

The single most common practice described among the 25 case studies was that of training. Such training could be grouped under several different headings.

Training directed at the migrants/ethnic minorities themselves

Historically, in many countries, training of the migrants themselves was the first type of activity adopted. Generally this was training for newcomers, teaching them the language, introducing them to important legal or cultural aspects of the new society, or showing them how to operate in the labour market. It was assumed that this would facilitate the integration of immigrants into society, and is still the sort of training given in many countries to refugees and other newcomers.

However, this was not the sort of training emphasised most in the case studies of the Compendium, which were generally dealing with an older and more established immigrant population. There were several examples of training directed quite specifically at the needs of a particular organisation, in two contexts:

1. Where restructuring of the economy has led to the closure of old industries and heavy unemployment amongst immigrant workers, who had been over-represented in these employment sectors.
2. Where restructuring within a firm has affected the existing immigrant workforce.

Examples can be given of each of these in turn. The first is ElectroCoat-Genk in Belgium, a subsidiary of one of the world's biggest electrocoating businesses. The company recruited via an agency set up to provide assistance to unemployed miners in the region, which had been in recession since the closure of the local coal mines. Only people who were 'just about employable' on the labour market were sought out. The training consisted of six months' familiarisation on the shop floor, and included technical training, working attitude and disposition, language mastery and intercultural co-operation. The aim in the firm was to establish among the multi-ethnic workforce a working climate in which each employee feels respected and has a sense of belonging to the firm. Workers of Maghrebian origin can take a longer leave period in the summer months if they put in a request to do so, and those who wish to pray can withdraw to the changing rooms to do so during breaks. One advantage gained by the company was that staff turnover was reduced to around 15 per cent per year, which is fairly low for a firm of this kind.

The second example is that of iR3 Video International, Austria, where training was introduced because of internal restructuring. An imperfect knowledge of German by immigrant workers became a potential problem when production began to be restructured. Work teams were being formed with the authority to make semi-autonomous decisions about the production process, the organisation of time and the allocation of duties within the team. It was no longer sufficient for a production worker to be passively able to understand instructions. He or she had to communicate actively within the team, in order to contribute to the team's success. Therefore the company initiated German courses for employees, comprising three principal elements: grammar, communication skills, and information of relevance to work and the company. Courses were held to fit in with the times when shifts began and ended. All classes were held in the factory itself, to keep costs to a minimum and to keep down the time involved for participants. The language courses reduced the likelihood of an adverse effect on both production and safety through misunderstandings, and also reduced the risk of immigrant workers being replaced by others with a better knowledge of German.

These are two of the examples of training directed towards migrant workers. However, the question has to be asked as to whether these are, in the words of the Joint Declaration, preventing racism and xenophobia. It might conceivably be argued that if these measures help to reduce the over-representation of immigrants and ethnic minorities among the unemployed, or promote their broader and better employment, then they are tackling the roots of racism by undermining the idea that visible minorities are second class citizens, naturally suited for second class jobs. This, however, is at best only *indirectly* confronting racism.

There are problems in over-emphasising the role of the training of immigrants, or as seeing it as sufficient in itself. For one thing, training directed at immigrants carries with it the assumption that the problems they encounter are a result of their own deficiencies. Yet there is a great deal of evidence from all over Europe, some of it quoted in Chapter 1 of this Dossier, that well-educated migrants and ethnic minorities with no language problems at all suffer discrimination and exclusion from opportunities for which they are well qualified. It can therefore be argued that if you are aiming to counter racism, discrimination and xenophobia, then your training should logically be directed at those whose attitudes and actions cause the problem, ie members of the white majority population. There are several different examples of this in the Compendium, and these can be divided into those initiatives which aim to change attitudes, and those which attempt to change behaviour.

Training directed at the majority: attitude change

An example of an initiative to change majority attitudes is the 'Living with Foreigners' campaign set up jointly by the German social partners, the Deutscher Gewerkschaftstund (DGB) and the Bundesvereinigung der Deutschen Arbeitgeberverbände (BDA). This is targeted at around one million apprentices in German industry, using training packages and media materials aimed at countering attitudes of intolerance and xenophobia. The assumption behind this sort of campaign is that educational material and greater contact with people from other cultures can help to break down attitudes of racism and prejudice, and thereby reduce discrimination. Another example of the provision of educational material or information for the white national employees is the local authority in Århus, Denmark's second largest city. All employees were sent a newspaper *På lige fod* (On an Equal Footing) which presented success stories of ethnic minorities employed in the council, the positive benefits of working with others from different cultures, and so forth.

The implicit assumption here is that the production of this sort of information will help to reduce racist attitudes and thereby reduce resistance to employing migrants. It is assumed that attitudes can be changed in this way, and that attitude change will lead to changes in behaviour and practices. However, this assumption may well be naive. For one thing, racist attitudes and prejudices are unlikely to be changed simply by the provision of training and information. Secondly, it is quite possible for practices of racial discrimination to be carried out by someone who does not have racist attitudes. Therefore, it is argued that attempts to produce changes in people's *behaviour* are more fruitful than trying to change peoples attitudes.

Training directed at the majority: behavioural change

A number of initiatives in the Compendium place a greater importance on changing individual behaviour than attempting to change attitudes. These initiatives can be divided into two sorts: those which can be categorised as 'multicultural' in their approach, or those which work from an 'anti-discrimination' perspective.

Examples of initiatives with a multicultural emphasis are those which provide training for managers and supervisors in intercultural management, or training workers in intercultural cooperation or how to work in multicultural teams. For example, the Thyssen Stahl steel company in Germany provides training in 'leading multicultural teams', as well as providing Turkish courses for German workers wishing to learn the language either for job-related or personal reasons. Similarly in the Netherlands the Dr Sarphatihuus nursing home introduced mandatory 'intercultural management' courses for middle and senior managers to help counter their ignorance about the implications of working with a multicultural staff.

Again, although these initiatives are undoubtedly valuable, they are still only indirectly addressing racism and discrimination. A more direct approach calls for an anti-discrimination rather than a multicultural emphasis. This kind of training would include that introduced in Belgium as a result of the Code of Conduct for temporary employment agencies, signed by employers and trade unions in the temporary employment agency sector. A survey of agency staff had revealed that most received discriminatory requests from employers, ranging from requesting perfect bilingualism for manual occupations – regarded in the temporary staff sector as a kind of secret code for the exclusive selection of Belgian workers – to explicit requests not to be sent any foreigners. Both trade union and employers' representatives admit that the temporary employment sector is indeed beset with problems of racial discrimination. The training aimed to make staff aware of the problem of racial discrimination, and instructed them how to respond to employers who made discriminatory requests, and how to ensure that only functionally relevant requirements are taken into account when selecting temporary staff.

There were other examples in the Compendium of the anti-discrimination training of 'gatekeepers' and others whose activities could have a direct effect on the opportunities of ethnic minorities. Measures included training on fair recruitment and selection procedures, and how to comply with anti-discrimination legislation. Generally speaking, these initiatives work from the assumption that 'measures to prevent racism and xenophobia and promote equal treatment at the workplace' are to be directed at members of the majority society, not at the migrants themselves, given that problems of racism, xenophobia and unequal treatment are the product of the attitudes and practices of the majority, and the workings and structures of the majority institutions of society.

Positive action

Many of the initiatives listed in the Compendium are aimed at providing equal treatment by attempting to change attitudes and practices, and removing discriminatory barriers, so as to produce the level playing field. However, there is also a strong argument that equal treatment and the provision of a level playing field is not enough, and that action is needed over and above the simple provision of equal rights and the removal of discrimination. A range of measures is needed where the targets are the migrants themselves, and these fall under the heading of positive action (CRE 1985). They are based on the assumption that equal treatment is not going to be much use if migrants are starting from very different and disadvantaged positions, sometimes because of the operation of racism and xenophobia in the past. Positive action goes further than equal treatment. Whereas equal treatment would mean treating people who apply for jobs without discrimination, positive action means, for example, making an extra effort to encourage groups who might not normally apply. Therefore, positive action is in fact doing something extra for previously excluded minorities, something you are not doing for the national majority (see Blakemore and Drake 1996; Moore 1997).

Positive action still arouses negative reactions in some quarters. In its weakest sense, however, positive action could simply mean devoting extra resources to language and other training for immigrants in order to better equip them for work. This type of initiative is probably the single most common among all the case studies in the Compendium, and seems to arouse the least controversy. Indeed, such measures might not even be called positive action at all, but simply varying the distribution of resources according to need. Other measures which go further than equal treatment are those which accommodate the specific religious or cultural needs of minority groups within the organisation. Again, these are reasonably common among the case studies. Forms of positive action might include special recruitment initiatives, such as translating job advertisements into ethnic minority languages, placing advertisements in the ethnic minority press, or using statements to encourage applicants from minorities. An increasingly used measure is that of mentoring. This is intended to increase the retention of minorities once they have been recruited into the organisation.

One problem with positive action measures is that they are regularly confused with positive discrimination, and thereby arouse hostility (see Jewson et al 1992). This may be due to the image gained from the US: there the term affirmative action was initially used in the same way as positive action is here, but over the years the meaning shifted towards elements of 'preferential treatment' (see Glazer 1987). In the Compendium the closest there is to preferential treatment is in the Dutch case studies, which, under Dutch law, were allowed to announce that in the case of equally qualified applicants, they would choose the one from a minority background. However, this is still not a particularly strong form of preferential treatment as it does not entail any lowering of standards. Only a minority of case studies operated a whole package of equal opportunities measures, covering, for example, the range of suggested initiatives in the Florence 'Joint Declaration', as well as others, combined with some positive action. Examples of these in the Compendium were the case studies in the Netherlands, Sweden and the UK, which could be called organisational equal opportunity policies.

Organisational equal opportunity policies

The first example is that of Virgin Our Price, a subsidiary company of the WH Smith Group, whose high street stores sell a wide range of goods including music CDs and cassettes, videos, games, books, T-shirts, chart music and other such accessories. The Group management decided to carry out an employee profile audit of the 30,000 workforce. Personal information forms were issued to all employees including a request to self-nominate their ethnic origin. The audit showed that although the proportion of ethnic minorities employed was broadly in line with the size of the ethnic minority population nationally (just over 5 per cent), ethnic minorities were under-represented in the Group in middle management and senior positions.

Virgin Our Price has made an explicit commitment to redressing past disadvantage through the adoption of positive action measures. Recognising that certain groups within the community may be under-represented in the business as a whole or in particular parts of it, it made special efforts to ensure that opportunities are made known to those groups, and where appropriate that training is provided to enable members of those groups to compete on equal terms for the opportunities available.

To ensure that interview panels operate according to the company equal opportunity policy, all individuals who sit on recruitment and selection panels receive anti-discriminatory training, and one personnel representative is present at all interviews. Virgin Our Price has also introduced an anti-harassment policy. It states that a single serious incident of harassment can result in summary dismissal for gross misconduct.

The company states that its policy has a number of advantages, including:

- attracting the best from the pool of skills and talent which is becoming increasingly multi-racial and using people's potential to the full;
- ensuring that the company meets the needs of its current and potential customers effectively through a workforce that reflects the make-up of the communities which it serves, and providing a competitive edge in reaching and attracting alternative new markets;
- avoiding incurring the direct costs of racial discrimination: financial, reduced employee moral and commitment, and cost to the image of the organisation resulting from adverse publicity.

A second example of an organisational equal opportunity policy is that of the North Holland Department of the Directorate-General for Public Works and Water Management, part of the Ministry of Transport, Public Works and Water Management, which is the third largest ministry in the Netherlands. It is responsible for flood defences and water management, traffic, transport and communications.

The head of personnel believed that an organisation like the North Holland Department could not 'stand apart from society' (the Department is located within a highly multi-ethnic part of the Netherlands.) At the end of 1991, the Ministry of the Interior called upon all parties to add extra wording to advertisements recruiting personnel from outside to the effect that all other things being equal, priority would be given to ethnic minorities, as well as to women and disabled people. However, applications to the organisation from ethnic minorities were low, and a survey revealed that disillusionment was one of the main reasons for the low response to advertisements. The study also showed that recruitment of ethnic minorities required a less conventional approach: for example, the use of informal networks. Contacts were then initiated with migrant organisations and other relevant bodies to stimulate applications. Also, agreements were concluded with other temporary employment agencies that requests for temporary staff would be met in the first instance by candidates from one of the ethnic minorities.

In addition to diversifying the recruitment procedures, the Department held preliminary interviews with applicants of minority ethnic origin to ensure that they met the requirements of the job. During the preliminary interview information was given about the organisation and the procedure, and applicants were advised on how to improve their letters of application and CVs. Preliminary interviews created a relationship of trust, so that contact was maintained after the initial application and feedback was obtained on the progress of the procedure. During selection, personnel officers were careful to see that the correct procedures were followed in the case of applicants of minority ethnic origin and that improper arguments were not used to reject them. Line managers underwent training in selection skills to avoid bias in selection interviews, and there were information campaigns and meetings with Dutch non-immigrant staff to get across the message of the initiative, and to reduce any potential hostility to it. By 1 January 1996 the percentage of employees of minority ethnic origin was seven per cent, two per cent higher than the recommended target set by the national Civil Service plan. It was interesting that this policy was introduced through the commitment of senior staff using arguments of a social and moral nature. Unlike the previous example, this organisation was not trying to increase its appeal to a multicultural clientele.

The final example is that of Stockholm County Council (Stockholms Läns Landsting, SLL), which is responsible for the Greater Stockholm region. SLL's official aims are to see to it that the competence of highly-educated immigrants is utilised and, in co-operation with other authorities, to make available the support and education required to provide immigrants with work which matches their qualifications. In the healthcare sector it was stressed that special importance should be attached to making use of the language and cultural competence of staff. Bilingual employees should be regarded as a valuable resource. There are also a number of training projects. The Council is integrating cultural issues into internal training, examining the need for special educational materials for specific groups, or producing material for personnel education on the subject of cultural understanding. A course entitled 'Racism and Xenophobia at Work' has been provided for work supervisors, personnel with immigrant backgrounds and teachers from the healthcare college. SLL sees that its programme in the healthcare sector has provided a better kind of healthcare for a multicultural society, and also provides better job opport-unities for immigrants in Sweden.

These organisations in the UK, the Netherlands and Sweden had policies of a greater variety and strength than the case studies from other countries.[5] Between them they operated a whole range of different practices, including special advertisements, allowances for cultural difference, positive action training for immigrants, training for staff on how to recruit and select without discrimination, and procedures for penalising harassment, with progress

---

[5] A 1991 ILO report similarly saw these three countries as 'frontrunners' in the development of anti-discrimination legislation (Zegers de Beijl 1991 p2).

reviewed and monitored by statistics, and targets set relating to the long-term proportional representation of minorities. The accurate monitoring of their workforces over time allowed these organisations to review their progress and make appropriate policy changes, and indeed, the monitoring was able to demonstrate that they had progressed significantly towards a greater representation of ethnic minorities amongst their employees.

ALTERNATIVE APPROACHES

In some EU countries the sorts of policies described above are quite unknown. This might be for two main reasons – either because of differences in national ideologies, or because of differences in national circumstances.

Differences in national ideologies

There are clearly great differences, historically and culturally, in national responses to migration and ethnic diversity. Castles (1995) categorises the major policy responses to immigration and ethnic diversity found in different countries. These include:

- *differential exclusion:* immigrants are seen as guest-workers without full social and political rights (eg Germany, Austria, Switzerland, Belgium);
- *assimilation:* immigrants are awarded full rights but are expected to become like everyone else (eg France, the UK in the 1960s);
- *pluralism/multiculturalism:* immigrants have full rights but maintain some cultural differences (eg Canada, Australia, Sweden, the UK more recently).

These are 'ideal' types, and in reality there have been some tensions within them. The differential exclusion model was based on the desire to prevent permanent settlement, and has proved hard to maintain because it leads to social tension and contradicts the democratic principle of including all members of civil society in the nation-state. The case of Germany fits this model, although there has been a shift to assimilation policies in some areas, and some multicultural policies in education. In France, perhaps the best example of the assimilation model with its republican tradition of 'equal treatment for all', there has been a move to some elements of the pluralist model, and this has led to some difficulties because of contradictions between explicit goals and actual policies. In the UK in the 1950s and 1960s there was a sort of *laissez-faire* assimilation which moved to pluralist and multicultural models in the 1970s. There is now a mixture of assimilationist and pluralist policies, without a clear overall objective (Castles 1995).

These contrasting national approaches provide very different contexts in which the case studies are located, and the implications of such differences must be recognised and allowed for in an analysis of good practice. Often, the ideologies relating to these ideal types remain in official discourse, and are directly reflected in how policies on the treatment of migrants and ethnic minorities are expressed. In the UK, for example, debates on the forms that multiculturalism might take are a regular part of public debate in some sectors, and equal opportunities policies recognise ethnic difference (Jenkins and Solomos 1987). In France, the emphasis is on broader 'equal rights' policies as a means of avoiding discrimination for all citizens and workers, and initiatives to encourage the recruitment of migrants have been phrased not in terms of anti-discrimination or anti-racism policies for migrants, but as egalitarian approaches guided by a universalistic ideology (De Rudder et al 1995). There are also wide differences between European countries in the readiness to record and use data according to ethnic minority background. This ranges from the UK, where a question on ethnic background forms part of the official Census, and where ethnic monitoring within organisations is often used to evaluate the progress of policies, to France and Denmark, where the recording of racial or ethnic origin in official or private registration is legally restricted.

The question is whether the sorts of policies discussed earlier – equal opportunity policies at an organisational level, positive action, celebrating diversity – are only compatible with the pluralist or multicultural approach. An example of an initiative with a different emphasis is that of the French case study.

The French case

In France, to talk of measures in 'Anglo-Saxon' equal opportunities terms runs counter to established philosophies of universalistic treatment, with a resistance to dividing up the targets of policies by ethnic background. Practices which benefit ethnic minorities are more likely to do so indirectly, without being designed in ethnically-specific forms. Thus the French case study in the Compendium is of a very different character to the others. This case covers the staff recruitment and training policy of the Continent hypermarket in a large shopping complex recently opened in an urban area in Marseilles (Quartiers-Nord) suffering from many social problems: unemployment and insecure employment, low incomes, a high proportion of people on benefit, a high percentage of young people without any qualifications or training, and so on. There is a high percentage of foreigners and French citizens of foreign origin in this area. However, acknowledging ethnic origin in the context of social policy contradicts the predominant republican model in France, and so in this case this is side-stepped by applying measures based on a territorial definition of social problems.

A policy of 'local preference for recruitment' in the shopping complex was initiated after vociferous lobbying (and even occasional acts of violence) during the construction phase by local people, who had felt that they were not going to receive any benefit from the new shopping complex. A *Charte Emploi* (Employment Charter) was drawn up, in which all retailers wanting to open outlets at the centre were asked to sign, and under which they undertook to give priority for jobs to people living in districts close to the shopping centre ('provided they have the appropriate skills and abilities'). A training programme for Continent managers was instituted, entitled 'Sensibilisation à la problématique des Quartiers-Nord de Marseille' (Raising awareness of the problems of Marseilles' Quartiers-Nord). The idea was to make managerial staff familiar with the hypermarket's economic, social and cultural context, and also with its future employees. An agreement was made with a local agency to select particularly disadvantaged people from the Quartiers-Nord, and provide them with initial training to improve their chances of being employed at Continent. The agreed selection criteria for these people were that the person must otherwise have 'little hope of getting a job', and that priority should be given to those persons resident in one of the four public housing estates closest to the shopping centre.

Ninety people followed an initial skills/employability training programme, and individual mentoring of trainees was also provided. Altogether, Continent took on 58 of these 90 people 'blind', ie without having to undergo any further selection tests, before the store opened; they were employed under permanent contracts, albeit only part-time, after receiving a further two to three months' training from the enterprise. An agreement was made with the *Agence Locale pour l'Emploi* to make provision for the establishment of a 'one-stop-shop' for recruitment, and this was followed by a local public information campaign to announce the availability of the jobs. At the end of this process, more than 450 people, including 220 cashiers, were recruited and began the training provided by Continent in August and September 1996. When the store opened, a total of 489 new staff had been hired, and 95 per cent of locally recruited employees were, by February 1997, covered by permanent contracts of employment.

There were clear business advantages seen to result from this policy. In other parts of France many suburban hypermarkets are said to be like fortified camps, trying to repel local residents and, especially, gangs of youths. Indeed, it is often at shopping centres of this kind that urban riots have begun. In contrast, in this case the Grand Littoral Shopping Centre has been accepted as their own by local people. Contrary to the rumours about chronic crime in the area, the centre seems to suffer less than its counterparts in other areas. Most of the members of the security team have been recruited from among young people living on the neighbouring estates, and this has appeared to engender mutual respect between the guards and young people from the same districts. Management spoke of the high motivation and commitment of the employees, and an absenteeism rate of less than 3 per cent, as against a national average of 7–9 per cent.

Thus, in this French example there was something very similar to what the British or Dutch would call positive action – a policy targeted at an excluded group. Training was directed at local disadvantaged people to improve their chances of employment at the hypermarket, and when this was combined with the policy to give priority for jobs to people living in the districts close to the shopping centre – provided that they had 'appropriate skills and abilities' – this formed a strong and effective positive action policy which borders on positive discrimination. This was less controversial than it might have been because it was not openly framed as positive action for ethnic minorities, but for local people.

Differences in national circumstances

All the examples in the Compendium of equal opportunities initiatives in general, and anti-discrimination measures in particular, are found in countries of northern Europe. One reason for this lies in those differences in the legal status of migrants between different EU countries, characterised by the five main categories of legal status set out in Section 1. These reflect a continuum of rights ranging from full rights and privileges of citizenship in category 1 to relatively few rights in category 5. It is clear that the problem of discrimination in the labour market of countries in the EU differs according to the categories into which most of its migrant and minority ethnic workers fall. This will have corresponding implications for both employers' and trade unions' policies and practices on discrimination and equality.

In countries of northern Europe, migrants and ethnic minorities are more likely to be skewed towards the top groups of the five legal categories of worker. Here, migrants are longer established and issues of the second generation are important, with concern over the unjustified exclusion of young people of migrant descent from employment opportunities by informal discrimination on racial or ethnic grounds, and their over-representation in unemployment. In the UK, for example, most migrants and their descendants are found in group 1; the legal status of migrant workers is generally not a problem, and a major part of equal opportunities activity concerns tackling the informal discrimination which in practice reduces the opportunities of minority ethnic workers, either at the workplace or within a trade union. In other countries of northern Europe, a higher proportion of workers fall into group 3, suffering not only informal racial discrimination but also formal legal discrimination. Here, the first stage of any initiatives generally concern themselves with the sorts of exclusion related to naturalisation and citizenship issues. This has implications for the overtones of the concept of discrimination itself. In the UK there is an acceptance of a broad definition of discrimination which allows for measures which tackle indirect, institutional or unintentional discrimination. In other countries of northern Europe such as Germany, avoiding discrimination is more likely to be seen narrowly as working to ensure equal employment rights, and paying equal wages for equal work, through formal agreements between the social partners.

In countries of southern Europe immigrants are likely to be over-represented towards the bottom of the five groups. Groups 4 and 5 workers are actively preferred and recruited because they are cheaper, more vulnerable, and more pliable – they are less able to resist over-exploitation in terms of work intensity or working hours, in conditions which indigenous workers would not tolerate. Anti-discrimination activities in these circumstances are initially more likely to emphasise measures to empower such workers and reduce their vulnerability to exploitation, with, for example, initiatives to unionise, regularise and train them.

Thus a practice within one context might carry different overtones to the same practice in another. For example, in a sector within a southern European country where migrants are severely exploited in illegal work because they do not have the power to resist or to seek alternative employment, providing language training for them in the national language might be seen to be part of anti-discrimination activity because it empowers them and enables them to resist such discrimination. In a country of northern Europe where migrants are longer established, including a second generation, the provision of language training is less likely to be seen as countering discrimination, and might even be interpreted as an 'alibi' for the absence of stronger measures.

In the UK most immigrants have full citizenship rights, often with a knowledge of English from colonial links, and are relatively long established in the country, with second and third generations being born. Here, equal opportunities policies and tackling informal discrimination directed at the second generation are valid. However, such instruments are less relevant for countries of southern

Europe where a newer migrant population is concentrated more towards the bottom groups – many are on restricted work permits, many are illegal, and most are relatively recent. To talk about 'ethnic monitoring' or 'targets' in an environment where large numbers of undocumented workers suffer great exploitation would be inappropriate. Here, simply implementing equal treatment would bring considerable improvements.

This difference in emphasis was borne out in the Compendium case studies from southern Europe, where many of the initiatives were directed to countering the inequality which is rooted outside the organisation, in broader society. Hence in Greece and Portugal, the case studies consisted of initiatives against the illegal exploitation of immigrants. In an Italian case study employers directed some of their measures outside the organisation with interventions to counter discrimination in the housing market on behalf of their employees, whilst in Spain the unions became concerned with broader welfare issues outside the workplace. Anti-discrimination initiatives in the forms found in, for example, the UK and the Netherlands, are less appropriate for these circumstances. Having said this, there was evidence of a growing realisation that in the future, employers and unions will need to take on board some of the ideas current further north in Europe. At the moment, immigrants in the southern countries of Europe are not generally in competition with native workers for their jobs. However, a whole new set of problems will arise when second generation immigrants with better academic qualifications and aspiring to more skilled work start to compete with the majority population in the normal labour market.

Differences in legal measures against discrimination

The strength of the law against employment discrimination provides an important context for the introduction of policies at an organisational level on equal opportunity. In some European countries there is very little legal pressure on employers; in some others there is recently enacted legislation against racial discrimination in employment, the effects of which cannot yet be properly judged. Even when strong law exists in theory, there can be problems in practice. The case of France is an example where a number of problems are experienced with the use of the criminal law against racism and discrimination. Cases of employment discrimination are seldom brought to court for lack of concrete evidence, and in practice employers are free to take on whoever they like, provided they do not openly show that the decision was based on criteria prohibited by law. Similarly in Sweden, from more than 100 cases of alleged discrimination in employment reported to the Ombudsman after the introduction of the law against discrimination in employment, none found their way to the courts. In the Netherlands a recent law commits companies with more than 35 employees to aim for the proportional representation of 'non-natives' in their workforces, and this puts pressure on them to formulate policies to achieve this. In theory, therefore, there is now more legal pressure in the Netherlands to institute such policies than in any other EU member state. There is thus a great deal of variety between different EU countries on the degree of background pressure to introduce policies for the prevention of racial discrimination and the promotion of equal treatment.

This point leads us to the question of whether more legal compulsion at EU level is necessary to get national laws into shape. Employers are generally against the idea of such legally-based pressure to introduce equal opportunity policies. Michael Banton writes:

> One of the reasons for resisting equal opportunities measures is that they entail changes to traditional assumptions ... and introduce external rules into what have previously been self-regulating processes. They extend

> *the sphere of public control and diminish that of private arrangement* (Banton 1994 p67).

This constitutes another example of the moving boundary between the private and the public sphere: once car drivers thought that drinking alcohol was a private concern, smokers thought they could smoke anywhere and motor cyclists thought that it was entirely their own business as to whether they wore a crash helmet or not:

> *Such things are now regarded as a matter of public concern and there are vigorous debates as to where the line between private and public should be drawn* (Banton 1994 p68).

Most European employers remain intrinsically and temperamentally opposed to legal constraint in this field. An awareness of the possibility of further legal measures was probably one of the factors which pushed European employers and trade union representatives towards agreement on the Joint Declaration on the Prevention of Racial Discrimination and Xenophobia and Promotion of Equal Treatment at the Workplace in 1995, which had the stated aim of encouraging more 'voluntary' initiatives in this field.

THE BUSINESS CASE FOR ACTION

Given the general resistance exhibited by European employers to the introduction of specific measures against racism and discrimination, it seems that the Joint Declaration will have to operate in an unsympathetic environment. The *European Compendium of Good Practice* showed that whilst progress is being made, the 'good practice' which exists is still somewhat 'tame'. The task would be greatly assisted if reluctant employers could be convinced that there is a business advantage in equal opportunity practices.

There may be a number of reasons why an individual employer might decide to introduce specific measures to counter discrimination and to further equal opportunities at the workplace, over and above the desire to reduce the likelihood of unlawful behaviour occurring within the organisation in countries where there is legislation against discrimination. There may be a calculation of commercial advantage by making the company more attractive to ethnic minority clients, improving the company image in a culturally diverse area, or improving the company's access to international markets. It may form part of an internal labour market policy to maximise the potential of existing valued employees, avoiding, for example, the poor motivation and low productivity that stems from workers employed below their capacity. Or it may be motivated by broader moral and social concerns over the divisions in the social fabric which may result from unwarranted exclusion from opportunities of one section of the community. Furthermore, the introduction of a well-managed equal opportunities programme which includes the accurate monitoring of both the existing workforce and new applicants can give new and helpful insights into aspects of the organisation's human resource management.

The case studies in the Compendium which operated a whole range of related equal opportunities measures also subscribed to a range of the above reasons. In several cases the good practice was initiated by individuals with a broader moral and social concern over the divisions in the social fabric which may result from unwarranted exclusion from opportunities of one section of the community, although often these concerns were mixed with the recognition that other practical benefits would also result.

Other practices, however, were driven primarily by a narrower and more immediate business imperative. For example, in some cases in the metal industry the institution of special language and vocational training for immigrants, and making allowance at work for cultural or religious practices, was driven primarily by the need to attract and retain immigrants in a sector where it was otherwise difficult to recruit workers. The case studies clearly show that in different ways and at different levels, many organisations perceive there to be direct and tangible business advantages in operating equal opportunities measures. In some cases the recognition of the benefit of the policies came from the approach of 'managing diversity', which argues vigorously in favour of the 'added value' which a mixed workforce can provide.

It is true that there can be identifiable advantages for an employer in the introduction of equal opportunity measures, and that in some EU member states some individual employers have embraced them willingly. However, the business argument can be overstated. Michael Rubenstein, writing in *Equal Opportunities Review* (Rubenstein 1987) calls the argument that equal opportunities makes good business sense a 'modern myth and misconception'. He argues that if this really were the case, then profit-maximising employers would have rushed to adopt policies years ago. The problem is that, far from being irrational, under some circumstances racial discrimination can be quite rational behaviour. Equal opportunities procedures cost time and money, and taking on a black employee instead of a white employee might impose a cost in terms of customer behaviour. Mark Gould, writing in the US, argues that although institutional racism may well be a characteristic of an inefficient system, organisations manifesting racism can nevertheless be competitive within the current institutional context because it lowers wages and reduces costs, even though alternative institutional arrangements would enhance the efficiency of production. Thus institutional racism can be profitable and sustainable for individual employers even though its elimination would lead to a more efficient and prosperous economy (Gould 1991). Rubenstein concludes that although equal opportunities are morally, socially and politically right, most employers will continue to discriminate until it costs them more to discriminate than not to discriminate, whether through financial sanction, the threat of law, or loss of commercial contract. Something similar was concluded after a major study of employers' equal opportunities practice, financed by the UK Department of Employment. The researchers concluded that a successful policy needed to have the commitment of organisational power holders such as senior directors, but that this commitment was unlikely to be 'voluntarily' secured without some sort of pressure. They argued that there were a number of ways in which this might be felt, such as moral pressure and example from government; financial incentives, such as those entailed in contract compliance; legal sanctions and penalties; and the emergence of perceived business advantage. Most of the initiatives they encountered in their research had their origins in outside pressures, such as urban disturbances or accusations of malpractice. A significant number of managers also told the researchers that as equal opportunities were costly in time and resources, they would be inclined to do more if there were a business advantage, or, more frequently, a discernible price to be paid for inaction (Jewson et al 1992; Jewson et al 1995).

The conclusion has to be that little progress is to be made if the major thrust of policy development in this area is left to such notions as 'equal opportunities are good for business'. Where a business pay-off is not immediately obvious, some extra pressure will need to be applied via the legal framework.

CONCLUSION

Chapter 1 of this Dossier set out the evidence for formal and informal discrimination in employment across countries of the EU. Chapter 2 considered the range of policy initiatives implied by this, at the level of both the

EU and individual member states. However, many of these policy options – EU action on the improvement of third country nationals, an EU directive against racial discrimination, as well as the improvement of citizenship rights and the introduction of effective anti-discrimination laws in many member states – are constrained by political opposition. The policy area less constrained in this way concerns those more 'voluntary' initiatives taken at the level of individual organisations, and directed at informal racial or ethnic discrimination. Thus Chapter 3 of the Dossier focused on examples of these initiatives in various European member states.

There has been some progress on these issues in recent years. The Joint Declaration on the Prevention of Racial Discrimination and Xenophobia and Promotion of Equal Treatment at the Workplace, signed in 1995 by EU workers' and employers' organisations, has had an educational impact helping to put the issue of racism and discrimination at work onto national agendas, in some countries for the first time. The 1997 European Year Against Racism provided a further stimulus to awareness on these issues. Nevertheless, it is clear that specific initiatives and measures by employers to counter racism, discrimination and the exclusion of migrants and their descendants are still not accorded the legitimacy they deserve in member states of the EU. The European Compendium gives some examples of positive practices, demonstrating the sorts of measures that might be adopted by others. However, when these are set in a broader EU context they remain untypical. One of the continuing rationalisations for inaction, frequently encountered at international meetings, is the argument that within a particular member state the problem of racism and discrimination in employment is abnormal and not widespread enough to justify the introduction of special measures. There is a common attitude of 'no problem here', an attitude which is, however, expressed uncommonly, each manifestation being culturally and historically specific to each member state. Examples of such national arguments expressed in recent years by employers' representatives, trade unionists, civil servants and officials are as follows:

- In Spain there is no racism towards migrants because Spain has traditionally been a country of *emigration*, and therefore its population understands well the problems faced by immigrants.
- Racism is not a normal part of Italian culture. This is apparent for two reasons: firstly, because Italian fascism, unlike German fascism, was never anti-Semitic, and secondly, because Italy had the largest communist party in Europe, reflecting a culture of international brotherhood and solidarity.
- In Germany racism is no longer a problem. Germany had been the most institutionally racist state in Europe under the Nazis, and therefore, racism was removed when the Nazi state was abolished.
- Racism is absent from French culture because since the 1789 revolution and the institutionalisation of 'liberty, equality and fraternity' into French society, France is the only European country which exhibits the true republican spirit of universalism.
- Racism is not a part of Swedish society because Sweden, unlike the major migrant-receiving countries of Europe, has never been a colonial power ruling over non-white peoples.
- In the Netherlands, racism is not a normal part of the national character because, in comparison to other European colonial powers, the Dutch operated a more benevolent form of colonialism. This is illustrated amongst other things by a high rate of inter-marriage between Dutch and ex-colonial peoples.
- Attitudes of racism are alien to the Portuguese character because Portugal was the first country to open up new lands with its voyages of discovery to Africa and India, thus exposing the Portuguese people

to non-Europeans earlier than other countries, and laying the foundations of universalism and tolerance in the national character.

Participants in international meetings have even heard the observation that the absence of legislation against racial discrimination in a particular country is in itself a convincing demonstration that the problem does not exist in that country.[6]

The evidence set out in Section 1 of this paper counters the assertion that there is 'no problem here', as well as showing that routine normal and institutional discrimination is not simply the result of extremists and right wing racists but is found quite commonly within the organisations of society. There is clearly a need to get racism and discrimination further on the European agenda, with specific measures to tackle them, even if the exact character of these measures will vary between different national contexts.

The European Compendium was not in any way a survey, simply a collection of case studies which act as examples of some of the practices at work. Therefore, it cannot be taken as providing an overview of the state of action on this issue across the EU. Nevertheless, it was significant that sometimes national researchers had to look rather hard to find their 'case studies of good practice' for the Compendium. Furthermore, many of those that were found could be characterised as rather tame. In some quarters there remains a ubiquitous assumption that measures to promote equal treatment in the labour market are to be directed at the migrants themselves, whilst those initiatives which are directed at the white majority frequently work from the assumption that racism and discrimination can be addressed simply by attitude change

---

6 The above arguments have all been heard by the author expressed at international conferences and meetings over recent years, apart from the Italian case, which was taken from documentary sources.

measures such as information provision, or a modicum of inter-cultural contact. Stronger anti-discrimination or anti-harassment measures which have implications for organisational practice are relatively rare.

One problem is that, on the whole, employers and their organisations remain ideologically unsympathetic to stronger measures to counter discrimination and to further equal opportunities. Receptivity to them seems to be greater in the public sector, and in the retail part of the private sector where a pay-off in terms of broader customer appeal is recognised. The business case for such measures remains unrecognised in some member states. Yet the business case itself can be overstated, and will not alone provide sufficient incentive for change. For this there is a need for the pressure of some external encouragement, such as national legislation, and to encourage this in turn there is a need for pressure from the European level.

There remains a resistance by some governments in the EU to act on the introduction or strengthening of legislation against racism and discrimination covering employment, either in their own country or at EU level. The opposition to action at EU level does not necessarily come from the same quarters as those who oppose it at their own national level. For example, until the election of the Labour government in 1997, the UK strongly opposed any action on this issue at EU level, even though the UK had the strongest anti-discrimination legislation in Europe. In the 1997 Treaty of Amsterdam an article which condemns discrimination based on criteria which include racial or ethnic origin was included for the first time. When this treaty is ratified, the European Commission will be empowered to propose appropriate action to combat this discrimination. Although this is progress, the article has been criticised because it says only that the Commission *may* act, rather than *must* act. Whilst action against racism and discrimination in organisations within EU member states remains truly voluntary, change is likely to remain slow.

References

Abell, J.P., Groothoff, M.C. and Houweling, I.L.M. (1985) *Etnische minderheden bij de overheid*, Amsterdam: ISBP

AMS (1991) *Arbetsförmedling som informationskanal bland arbetsökande. Rapport från Utredningsenheten*, Stockholm: AMS

Banton, M. (1994) *Discrimination*, Buckingham: Open University Press

Bauböck, R. (1992) *Immigration and the Boundaries of Citizenship*, Monographs in Ethnic Relations No.4, Warwick: University of Warwick

Becker, H.M. and G.J. Kempen (1982) *Vraag naar migranten op de arbeidsmarkt*, Rotterdam: Erasmus Universiteit Rotterdam

Blakemore, K. and Drake, R. (1996) *Understanding Equal Opportunity Policies*, London: Prentice Hall/Harvester Wheatsheaf

Bovenkerk, F. and E. Breunig-van Leeuwen (1978) 'Rasdiscriminatie en rasvooroordeel op de Amsterdamse arbeidsmarkt' in: F. Bovenkerk (ed) *Omdat zij anders zijn; patronen van rasdiscriminatie in Nederland*, Meppel: Boom

Bovenkerk, F. (1986) *Een eerlijke kans. Over de toepasbaarheid van buitenlandse ervaringen met positieve actie voor etnische minderheden op de arbeidsmarkt in Nederland*, Den Haag: Ministerie van Binnenlandse Zaken, Ministerie van Sociale Zaken en Werkgelegenheid

Bovenkerk, F. (1992) *Testing Discrimination in Natural Experiments: A Manual for International Comparative Research on Discrimination on the Grounds of 'Race' and Ethnic Origin*, Geneva: International Labour Office

Bovenkerk, F., Gras, M.J.I. and Ramsoedh, D. (1995) *Discrimination against Migrant Workers and Ethnic*

65

Minorities in Access to Employment in the Netherlands, Geneva: International Labour Office

Brandt, B. (forthcoming) 'The Policy of Exclusion: The German Concept of Citizenship' *Migration*, Sondernummer

Burstein, P. (1992) 'Affirmative Action, Jobs and American Democracy: What Has Happened to the Quest for Equal Opportunity', *Law and Society Review*, 26 (4)

Cachón, L. (1995) *Preventing Racism at the Workplace: Report on Spain*, Dublin: European Foundation for the Improvement of Living and Working Conditions

Campani, G., Carchedi, F. Mottura, G. and Pugliese, E. (1995) *Preventing Racism at the Workplace in Italy*, Dublin: European Foundation for the Improvement of Living and Working Conditions

Carlos, M.L.P. and Borges, G.C. (1995) *Preventing Racism at the Workplace in Portugal*, Dublin: European Foundation for the Improvement of Living and Working Conditions

Castles, S. (1995) 'How nation-states respond to immigration and ethnic diversity' *New Community* 21 (3) July

Colectivo IOE: M. Angel de Prada, W. Actis, C.Pereda and R. Pérez Molina (1996) *Labour market discrimination against migrant workers in Spain*, Geneva: International Labour Office

CEC (1993) *Legal Instruments to Combat Racism and Xenophobia*, Luxembourg: Commission of the European Communities, Office for Official Publications of the European Communities

CRE (1985) *Positive Action and Equal Opportunity in Employment*, London: Commission for Racial Equality

Cross, M., Wrench, J., and Barnett, S. (1990) *Ethnic Minorities and the Careers Service: An Investigation into Processes of Assessment and Placement*, London: Department of Employment Research Paper No.73

Coussey, M. and Hammelburg, H. (1994) *A Code of Practice to Combat Racial Discrimination and to Promote Equal*

Opportunities at Work Volume 1, Brussels: European Human Rights Foundation

Denolf, L. and Martens, A. (1991) *Van 'mijn'werk naar ander werk: Onderzoeksrapport over de arbeidsmarkpositle van ex-mijnwerkers*, Brussels: Permanente Werkgroep Limburg

De Rudder, V., Tripier, M. and Vourc'h, F. (1995) *Prevention of Racism at the Workplace in France*, Dublin: European Foundation for the Improvement of Living and Working Conditions

Drew, D., Gray, J. and Sime, N. (1992) *Against the Odds: The Education and Labour Market Experiences of Black Young People*, Sheffield: Employment Department Research and Development Paper No.68

Dummett, A. (1994) *Citizens, Minorities and Foreigners: A guide to the EC*, London: Commission for Racial Equality

Ekholm, E. and Pitkänen, M. (1995) *Preventing Racism at the Workplace in Finland*, Dublin: European Foundation for the Improvement of Living and Working Conditions

Fakiolas, R. (1995) *Preventing Racism at the Workplace in Greece*, Dublin: European Foundation for the Improvement of Living and Working Conditions

Forbes, I. and Mead, G. (1992) *Measure for Measure*, London: Employment Department Research Series No. 1

Gächter, A. (1995) *Preventing Racism at the Workplace in Austria*, Dublin: European Foundation for the Improvement of Living and Working Conditions

Glazer, N. (1987) *Affirmative Discrimination: Ethnic Inequality and Public Policy*, Cambridge, Massachusetts: Harvard University Press

Goldberg, A., Mourinho, D. and Kulke, U. (1995) *Labour market discrimination against foreign workers in Germany*, Geneva: International Labour Office

Gras, M. and Bovenkerk, F. (1995) *Fighting Discrimination and Ethnic Disadvantage on the Dutch Labour Market*, Dublin: European Foundation for the Improvement of Living and Working Conditions

Groenendijk, K. and Hampsink, R. (1995) *Temporary Employment of Migrants in Europe*, Nijmegen: Reeks

Recht and Samenleving Nr.10, Katholieke Universiteit Nijmegen

Gould, M. (1991) 'The Reproduction of Labour-Market Discrimination in Competitive Capitalism' in A Zegeye, L. Harris and J. Maxted (eds), *Exploitation and Exclusion: Race and Class in Contemporary US Society* London: Hans Zell

Hammar, Tomas (1990) *Democracy and the Nation State: Aliens, Denizens and Citizens in a World of International Migration*, Aldershot: Avebury

Hjarnø, J. (1995) *Preventing Racism at the Workplace: The Danish national report*, Dublin: European Foundation for the Improvement of Living and Working Conditions

Hjarnø, J. and Jensen, T. (1997) 'Diskrimineringen af unge med invandrerbaggrund ved jobsøgning', *Migration papers* No. 21, Esbjerg: South Jutland University Press

Hubbuck, J. and Carter, S. (1980) *Half a Chance? A Report on Job Discrimination against Young Blacks in Nottingham*, London: Commission for Racial Equality

Jenkins, R. (1986) *Racism and Recruitment*, Cambridge: Cambridge University Press

Jenkins, R. and Solomos; J. (1987) *Racism and Equal Opportunity Policies in the 1980s*, Cambridge: Cambridge University Press

Jewson, N. and Mason, D. (1991) 'Economic Change and Employment Practice: Consequences for Ethnic Minorities' in M. Cross and G. Payne (eds) *Work and the Enterprise Culture*, London: Falmer

Jewson, N., Mason, D., Lambkin, C. and Taylor, F. (1992) *Ethnic Monitoring Policy and Practice: A Study of Employers' Experiences*, London: Department of Employment Research Paper No.89

Jewson, N., Mason, D., Drewett, A. and Rossiter, W. (1995) *Formal Equal Opportunities Policies and Employment Best Practice*, London: Department for Education and Employment, Research Series No.69

Kloek, W. (1992) *De positie van allochtonen op de arbeidsmarkt*, Heerlen: Centraal bureau voor de statistiek

Kollwelter, S. (1995) *Preventing Racism at the Workplace in Luxembourg*, Dublin: European Foundation for the Improvement of Living and Working Conditions

Layton-Henry, Z. (1990) (ed) *The Political Rights of Migrant Workers in Western Europe*, London: Sage

Lee, G. and Wrench. J. (1983) *Skill Seekers – Black Youth, Apprenticeships and Disadvantage*, Leicester: National Youth Bureau

Lyon-Caen, G. (1992) *Les libertés publiques et l'Emploi*, Paris: Rapport au Ministre de Travail, de l'emploi et de la formation professionelle, La Documentation Française

MacEwen, M. (1995) *Tackling Racism in Europe*, Oxford: Berg

MacEwen, M. (ed) (1997) *Anti-Discrimination Law Enforcement: A Comparative Perspective*, Aldershot: Avebury

Mirza, Q. (1995) *Race Relations in the Workplace*, London: The Institute of Employment Rights

Moore, R. (1997) *Positive Action in Action*, Aldershot: Ashgate

Paulson, S. (1991) *Utvecklingsbehov för framtidens arbetskraft. En studie om invandrare på Göteborgs arbetsmarknad*, Göteborg: Göteborgs Näringslivssekrateriat

Rogstad, J. (1995) *Preventing Racism at the Workplace: The Norwegian National Report*, Dublin: European Foundation for the Improvement of Living and Working Conditions

Rubenstein, M. (1987) 'Modern Myths and Misconceptions: 1 "Equal Opportunities Makes Good Business Sense"' *Equal Opportunities Review* 16 November–December

Sales R. and Gregory J. (1995), 'Employment, citizenship and European integration : the implications for migrant and refugee women', Paper presented at the Annual Conference of the British Sociological Association, April 1995 (A revised version of this article was later published in *Social Politics* 3 (2/3) 1996)

Schaub, G. (1993) *Rekrutierungsstrategien und Selektionsmechanismen für die Ausbildung und die Beschäftigung junger Ausländer*, BIBB: Berlin

Soininen M. and Graham, M. (1995) *Persuasion Contra Legislation. Preventing Racism at the Workplace: The Swedish national report*, Dublin: European Foundation for the Improvement of Living and Working Conditions

SOU (1995) *Arbete till invandrare*, Stockholm Delbetänkande från Invandrarpolitiska kommittén

Speller, T. and A. Willems (1990) *Scholing en arbeidsmarktpositie van allochtonen*, Nijmegen: Katholieke Universiteit Nijmegen

Van Beek, K. (1993) *To be Hired or not to be Hired: The Employer Decides*, Amsterdam: University of Amsterdam

Veenman, J. (1985) *De werkloosheid van Molukkers*, Den Haag: Ministerie van Sociale Zaken en Werkgelegenheid

Veenman, J. (ed.) (1990) *Ver van huis: achterstand en achterstelling bij allochtonen*, Groningen: Wolters-Noordhoff

Verweij, A.O. (1991) 'Gelijke kansen voor allochtonen op ontslag? Een onderzoek naar uitstroom van allochtone werknemers', *Migrantenstudies*, 1

Wrench, J. and Solomos, J. (eds) (1993) *Racism and Migration in Western Europe*, Oxford: Berg

Wrench, J. (1996) *Preventing Racism at the Workplace: A report on 16 European countries*, Luxembourg: Office for Offical Publications of the European Communities

Wrench, J. (1997) *European Compendium of Good Practice for the Prevention of Racism at the Workplace*, Luxembourg: Office for Offical Publications of the European Communities

Zegers de Beijl, R. (1991) *Although equal before the law... The scope of anti-discrimination legislation and its effects on labour market discrimination against migrant workers in the United Kingdom, the Netherlands and Sweden*, Geneva: International Labour Office

Zegers de Beijl, R. (1995) 'Labour market integration and legislative measures to combat discrimination against migrant workers' in *The integration of migrant workers in the labour market: Policies and their impact*, W.R.Böhning and R. Zegers de Beijl, Geneva: International Labour Office

Other Titles
in the Series

Other titles available in the series include:

Unemployment and Employment Policies in the EU
Secrecy, Democracy and the Third Pillar of the European Union
The 1996-97 Intergovernmental Conference
The Politics of the European Court of Justice
EU-East Asia Economic Relations: Completing the Triangle?
Ukraine and the EU
Social Europe: A New Model of Welfare?
Alternative Paths to Monetary Union
Gender and Citizenship in the EU
Britain and European Integration: An Overview

Further information on all titles in the series is available from the publishers at the undermentioned address:

Kogan Page Limited
120 Pentonville Road
London N1 9JN